CHAMPIONS

Application of Common Sense and Biblical Motifs to Excel in Both Worlds

Charles Mwewa

ACP – Ottawa
2021

ISBN: 978-1-988251-48-6

DEDICATION

For

Felix Kazwala

R.I.P.

CONTENTS

INTRODUCTION

The Bible, and Jesus in particular, dealt with everyday social realities in a manner that confounded even the best and brilliant minds of the time. Common-sense is very much at play in most of the biblical themes, stories and encounters. The unified consensus of the Scriptures points to the same conclusion: That God wants us to win in both worlds, in this, and in the one to come.

Biblical characters did not exist in a vacuum; they were real people who faced real challenges and joys of life. And from the selected passages compiled here, there is irrefutable evidence that everything God made is full of wisdom – it is the humans' job to find that wisdom, even in the activities of tiniest insects. The content of this book can be summed up in this wise:

- A beggar teaches balance;

- Investing in talents is profitable;
- Being good at what one does, attracts promotion;
- There is power in rankings;
- It's normal to gain wealth but unwise to worship it;
- Each person's gift is the key to everything they desire;
- "Money answers all things," but it is not the answer to the most important things;
- Slaves of good things are masters over bad things;
- Work is the most basic blessing to all of humanity;
- Humans may be political animals but participation can be through any good means;
- Sometimes smartness can mix with poison just as innocence can be duplicitous;
- Position without possession may be a drudge;
- There must be equal pay for equal value, always;

- Rock badgers are not a mighty people, but they make their homes in the rocks;
- Locusts have no king, yet they advance together in ranks;
- Lizards are easy to catch, but they are found even in kings' palaces; and
- Ants are creatures of little strength, yet they store up their food in the summer.

In the Bible, it is written, "It is the glory of God to conceal things, but the glory of kings is to search things out."[1] Here lies the power of wisdom – God reveals things by hiding them; humans reach their highest glory by searching those things out. Everything God wants us to know is somewhere hidden, and it is our task to research and find it. The Bible could best be described as *the revelations of revelation.* In it, God has hidden wisdom nuggets and intelligent wits through anecdotes, sayings of wisdom, songs, proverbs,

[1] Proverbs 25:2

parables, fables, allegories, tales, metaphors, and even in skirmishes, confrontations and struggles. It is our job to find out the meaning and then apply it to our practical lives.

This book highlights some of those hidden gems. All those who desire to be champions, to win, to excel, in this present world and to be welcomed with admiration in the next, will have found their match through the contents of this book.

1 DOUBLE COMFORT

"There was a rich man who was dressed in purple and fine linen and lived in luxury every day. At his gate was laid a beggar named Lazarus, covered with sores and longing to eat what fell from the rich man's table. Even the dogs came and licked his sores," (Luke 16:19-21).

There are five points to take home:

1. The complete story of "The Rich Man and Lazarus" is told by Jesus in Luke 16:19-31.[2]

2. The story has been over-explained from the spiritual angle; the story involves both the heavenly and earthly principles. In this dissertation, we consider it from its earthly perspective.

3. The "Rich Man" does not go

[2] See Appendix I at page 111

to Hell because he was rich; and "Lazarus" does not go to Heaven ("Abraham's bosom") because he was poor.

4. The "Rich Man" goes to Hell because he did not "repent" (verse 30), not because of his riches. If his riches contributed to his disobedience, the passage does not tell. What the passage infers is that even in his riches, if only he had also repented, he would have been in Heaven.

5. Lazarus goes to Heaven because he believed in the words of "Moses and the Prophets." There was no salvation through Jesus Christ in those days, faith was generated through the Law – Moses and the Prophets – and Lazarus believed. Lazarus doesn't go to Hell because of his poverty – that's not the inference drawn from this passage.

LESSON:

There are five lessons we can learn from this passage:

(1) Our status or position on earth does not impact our eternal foundation. What it does is, it impacts our choice to believe in God or not to believe. If we believed in God, no matter our station in life (rich or poor), we would be welcomed in God's eternal bliss. The rendition of "Again I tell you; it is easier for a camel to go through the eye of a needle than for someone who is rich to enter the kingdom of God,"[3] does not preclude the rich man from entering into Heaven, it only makes it a bit difficult. But as our Lord taught, "With man this is impossible, but with God all things are possible."[4]

(2) God does not discriminate against

---

[3] Matthew 19:24
[4] Matthew 19:26

the rich or the poor, God loves the rich person as much as He does the poor one.

(3) If you are rich in material things on earth, you can enjoy the good things of this world – good house, good car, luxury living, exotic apparel, flamboyant parties, and etc. If you are poor and lack material things you will struggle to make a living – you will probably beg or eat crumbs from the wealthy or worse. It is not God's problem that you are poor on earth, it's your choice. God does not judge you, either, for living large on earth, it's your industry, position and sometimes pure luck, that determines so.

(4) If you are a child of God, you can choose to live in luxury – that's perfectly fine with God. God Himself lives in unexplained splendor and glory in Heaven. But even if you were poor and yet a believer, God would still love you.

(5) Poverty is expected on earth,

note, "You will always have the poor among you,"[5] were the humble words of our Lord, but a believer's default position has been elevated to richness, "For you know the grace of our Lord Jesus Christ, that though he was rich, yet for your sake he became poor, so that you through his poverty might become rich."[6]

APPLICATION:

"Double Comfort" – is the state of being wealthy and comfortable here on earth while knowing that you will be comfortable in Heaven as well. It is simple to attain to "Double Comfort" as the Bible says, "Believe in the Lord Jesus, and you will be saved…"[7] Salvation secures your eternal comfort. However, to attain to earthly comfort, you have to be deliberate in your pursuit for wealth. Those who will be both saved and possess earthly wealth will be wiser and more useful on earth – to both God and men –

---

[5] Matthew 26:11
[6] 2 Corinthians 8:9
[7] Acts 16:31

than those who are only saved but poor on earth. In fact, being both spiritually saved and materially rich will enable you to do more for the Kingdom of God on earth – you can reach more people with the Gospel, you can build more facilities, advance more resources for missions, teach more, preach more, and etc. In short, a rich saved person has both the faith and the means to serve and worship God, while a poor saved person has the faith but limited means to impact their world for Jesus.

WISDOM TIP:

After salvation, aim to become wealthy so you can impact your world in a meaningful way. There are benefits of having money or wealth: You can do more for God. You can reach further places than if you are poor. You can help more people who are poor if you have the means to do so than if you don't have. The rich should use their money for godly purposes.

2 PROFIT-MOTIVATED

"Whoever has will be given more, and they will have an abundance. Whoever does not have, even what they have will be taken from them," (Matthew 13:12)

There are five points to take home:

1. The story of the talents is well illustrated in Matthew 25:29. In the passage in Matthew 25, three people are given three talents; one five sets of gold, another two sets of gold and still another one set.

2. Each was given according to their ability.[8] It was assumed that they had to invest their talents.

3. The master (owner of the wealth) did not tell them what to do with their talents.

---

[8] See Matthew 25:15

4. The two people with five and two talents, "traded" and gained twice as much. In other words, they made profit. The other person who had received one, buried it in the ground and did not "trade" it to make profit.

5. The master returned and demanded accounts of the wealth he had left. He promoted the two who made profits. The master condemned the one who buried the talents due to fear and indifference. The master called him, "lazy" and "wicked" and he was fired or demoted.

LESSON:

God has given each person something basic they can develop. God does not expect to tell you what to do with what He has given you, but He expects you to develop it and make profit. The talents are not only spiritual gifts; they cover all aspects of humanity, body, soul/mind and spirit. It is not God's job to tell you what to do; it is your duty to acknowledge your God-given gift and use it. God does not expect you to die raw – just the way you came into the world. God expects you to die bigger, greater, more prosperous and accomplished. No-one is born to decrease; people are born to increase. You should work to improve your body, sharpen your mind, and edify your spirit. You cannot remain basic and a "baby" all your life. you should make progress all the time.

APPLICATION:

(1) Nature behaves likewise. We are born as babies, and each day we are growing as we are cared for and tendered. If we are only left to grow unattended, we may probably die quickly.

(2) Vegetation and animals illustrate this principle further; they compete for space and livelihood to increase.

(3) If you don't care for your body, it will probably age fast and die young. It is your responsibility to "improve" your body – use anything that works to do so, creams, herbs, therapy, and etc. Do something to your body to look beautiful, youthful or handsome. If you have to pay money to improve yourself, please do so. Improve your home, your surroundings and your property. Gain more, achieve more and do more with your time, energy and talents.

(4) Improve your soul/mind. That is, challenge your brain to new knowledge and discoveries – read extensively, research widely and be fascinated with new things. Add to your knowledge all the time and do not simply rely on what you know. Explore multi-discipline understanding – don't just limit yourself to religion, know all other things (sciences, law, mathematics, communication, logic, psychology, sociology, technology, and etc.) God hasn't called you to be myopic but

bountiful. Go for knowledge and improve your understanding of the world.

(5) Develop your spirit – read the Bible, pray, follow God's commands, love all people and strive to do good to fellow humans and to animals and vegetation. Aim to be perfect as God is perfect.

(6) Increase your worth – buy property, work hard at your job, be creative in your business, and etc.

(7) Grow in outlook – connect more with people, communicate more and expose yourself more. In other words, do something not to die basic, empty and a nobody. Indeed, we all came naked and naked we will return – but that is true whether you are rich or poor, somebody or nobody and etc. What everyone should do is to grow yourself and though you will die naked, you will have left the legacy as one who developed what God gave them.

(8) Not developing what God gave you is laziness and could even be considered wickedness. It is, definitely, lacking in thanksgiving. Don't bury your talents, expand them.

WISDOM TIP:

God has put the ability to grow and buoy in every baby that is born. However, if the child is neglected, notwithstanding its ability to grow, the baby may die due to negligence. Nature may necessitate birth, but it's nurture that brings results. God, surely, has given you talents and abilities. They will remain nothing but potential unless you use and develop them.

3 BEAT THE COMPETITION

"Study to show yourself approved to [your boss, employer, competition, business, the world, and etc.], a workman that needs not to be ashamed, rightly dividing the word of truth," (2 Timothy 2:15)

There are five points to take home:

1. This verse is a principle: It can apply to any persuasion or area in life. Paul only uses it in the context of biblical economics. It can apply to your career, field of study, profession, ministry, business, and etc.

2. Study (or learning, training, education, perfecting your skills or acquiring a trade, and etc.). Like children who have to learn to talk even though the Language Acquisition Device (LAD) exists naturally in them, so should we in all

areas of life. Study perfects the raw materials we are born with. Everything we want to become has been deposited inside of us by divine providence. All we need to do is to studying and perfect them. Study or training expands our understanding of who we are and of those around us, our world.

3. Show yourself: This means to get others to see you. It is like walking on a catwalk – the world is watching and seeing you on its stage, just like God is watching you if this applies to ministry. Studying or training helps you to perfect your qualities and which makes you visible and attractive to those who need what you are or have. Show yourself also means to prove yourself, to excel.

4. When your perfected qualities come out with excellence, you

will be approved: Approval does not come by dreams or wishes, it comes by excelling. Be the best at what you do. Do your best…work hard…make every effort…be diligent…win the approval of – in other words, beat the competition.

5. Failure to study or be diligent has consequences: The person who fails to perfect their qualities will not achieve greatly – that is, they will be unsuccessful, average or below, sub-standard, poor, and the like.

LESSON:

It's amazing how people find excuses for failure. They own all successes and deflect failure and shame. Wisdom demands that we accept the benefits of success and we also accept the pain of failure.

First, the Bible does not discourage competition, even among the same fraternity. What the Bible is against is setting a human standard of success as a model. Christ is the standard. Thus, two believers can be compared so long as they aim to reach or exceed Christ's standard.

Second, our works can be compared – and this is the basis for receiving both earthly and eternal rewards. God will "judge" every labor done under the sun.

Third, to win human approval and adulation, our qualities and works are judged. Humans judge each other, and to succeed in the world, you must meet and exceed expectations in whatever you do in life. if you are a businessperson, meet and beat business expectations. If you are in academia, meet or exceed academic expectations; if you are an employee, meet and exceed your employment expectations; if you are in Gospel Ministry, strive to meet Christ's standard and it is absolutely right to try to beat the competition – as Paul said, "But what does it matter? The important thing is that in every way, whether from false motives or true, Christ is preached. And because of this I rejoice."[9]

Last, if you have good qualities or you have achieved what could be beneficial to many people, advertise yourself and seek to beat all competitions. In other words, show yourself approved – that you are skilled, gifted, talented and excellent in all you do.

If you do the above, you will:

(1) Easily be promoted wherever you are;

(2) Easily stand out among the competition;

(3) Have become a brand name – people will be seeking after you;

(4) Have your works be quoted by people;

---

[9] Philippians 1:18

(5) Have great connections and many important people will be attracted to your;

(6) Leave a legacy and leave behind an inheritance for your children; and

(7) Earn God's approval.

APPLICATION:

Three qualified and good Christian candidates apply for a General Manager job position. All of them pray to God to succeed in getting the job and God answers all the three of them. The interviewer/company only hires one of them. Was God unfair? No.

All of them prayed and God answered their prayers. When they attended the actual interviews, as far as God is concerned, they had their prayers answered; they had equal chances to getting that job.

One of them, though, beat the competition – she was probably better prepared, answered questions correctly, dressed more appropriately, sold her strengths intelligently, gave very good facial impressions and expressions, knew or had studied the nature of the interview or the history of that company or anything useful to use, and etc. You get the point? You can apply this to marriage proposals, business success, academic progress, ministry expansion, and the list is endless.

WISDOM TIP:

You can do anything if you take time to study and learn about it. The mind, the brain can expand only to the extent to which it is exercised. Studying strengthens the brain and improves the mind's versatility.

Not all knowledge is found in colleges and universities. You can teach yourself – by observing nature and human behavior. You can also learn on your own by borrowing books from libraries or from those who have home libraries. You can make use of free book resources and reading materials from the Internet. When you learn about something, you increase the chances of excelling in that discipline. Keep your mind filled with knowledge and be preoccupied with learning wherever you have the opportunity. If you don't have any opportunity, create one.

4 YOU'RE GOD'S BUSINESS

"Thus, says the LORD, 'Heaven is my throne, and earth is the footstool of my feet,'"
(Isaiah 66:1)

There are five points to take home:

1. A footstool is the place where the mortals bow or kneel to worship the deity or royalty: "Exalt the LORD our God; worship at his footstool! Holy is he!"[10]

2. A footstool is a place of humbleness, not honor. The lowly and enemies belong here: "The LORD said to my Lord, "Sit in the place of honor at my right hand until I humble your enemies, making them a footstool under your

[10] Psalm 99:5

feet."[11]

3. A footstool is a symbol of rest: "The throne had six steps, and a footstool of gold was attached to it. On both sides of the seat were armrests, with a lion standing beside each of them."[12]

4. A throne is a high chair for a deity, king, queen or emperor – it is a symbol of power.

5. A throne is a ceremonial posting – a deity, king, queen or emperor sits here to make judicial and other important decisions. It is a symbol of authority.

[11] Psalm 110:1

[12] 2 Chronicles 9:18

LESSON:

Relative to the heavens, the earth is only a footstool where God rests His feet. Heaven is His throne and has His throne. In terms of position, the earth is very low – only fit for lowliness and for God's enemies. In reality, God's children live on earth (under God's feet), but in terms of redemption, they live in the heavenlies with God.

Here are six important things to remember:

(1) Anyone who is out of Christ is at the bottom of the elevation and is susceptible to this world's system and to the devil.

(2) Anyone who is not in Christ is not with God; they are as chaff to be trodden upon.

(3) Anyone who is rich in worldly things only or whose interest is only in worldly things, has a temporary existence, limited joy, and no real power and authority.

(4) Whoever is in Christ, is by way of position, elevated in the heavenlies where Christ is also sited: "And God raised us up with Christ and seated us with him in the heavenly realms in Christ Jesus…"[13]

(5) Anyone who has spiritual wealth (love, faith, hope, character, justice, goodness, generosity, righteousness, grace, and etc.) is truly and permanently rich – because their position is far above in the heavenlies: "Blessed be the God and Father of our Lord Jesus Christ, who has blessed us in Christ with every spiritual blessing in the heavenly realms."[14]

(6) Anyone who is in Christ has a throne and a kingdom and they are, therefore, royalty: "And I appoint unto you a kingdom, as my Father hath appointed unto me…"[15]

---

[13] Ephesians 2:6
[14] Ephesians 1:3
[15] Luke 22:29,30

APPLICATION:

You should look at yourself this way in terms of position in Christ. Therefore, those who are on earth and are at the same time in Christ, have double advantage; they are on earth, but they are not really of this world. They can do everything every human being does on earth, but they can also experience the life of bliss and peace as it is in Heaven.

It is a matter of position; therefore, you must know when to stand on your throne and make demands, through the prayer of faith. Royalty does not beg, they demand. Royalty does not ask questions; they make statements and orders. And royalty must know they are royal otherwise none-entities will challenge them or usurp their power. ignorance is not a defence.

IMPLICATIONS:

Those who are in Christ are very powerful and have tremendous authority and access to everything in the heavenlies. But they must know and live likewise!

5 WEALTH OF WORSHIP

"Again, the devil took him to a very high mountain and showed him all the kingdoms of the world and their splendor. 'All this I will give you,' he said, 'if you will bow down and worship me.' Jesus said to him, 'Away from me, Satan! For it is written: Worship the Lord your God, and serve him only,'" (Matthew 4:8-10).

There are five points to take home:

1. When this statement was made, the devil had legitimate claim to all the kingdoms of the world and their splendor.

2. Whoever has legitimate claim to kingdoms has enormous power and influence. All men and women desire wealth, riches and what comes with such.

3. Call it flattery or making happy or worship, when you worship

the one who has kingdoms (wealth and riches), they will normally give you riches. That's one of the easiest ways of getting rich.

4. At that time, Jesus did not dispute what the devil said, namely, that all kingdoms and their splendor belonged to him. The devil was telling the truth, but, of course, with an ulterior motive.

5. After Jesus died and rose again, thus fulfilling God's redemption plan, God gave Him all the kingdoms of the world and their splendor, i.e., "Then Jesus came to them and said, 'All authority in heaven and on earth has been given to me.'"[16] Jesus has more authority and power than the devil; His permeates the heavens and the earth. The devil's was only in the world, and he lost it.

[16] Matthew 28:18

LESSON:

Jesus has revealed two ways in which we normally get wealth and money. We either worship someone important and powerful and in turn they reward us with wealth. Or we serve (render a service) to someone with means and in turn they pay us a salary.

We may get wealth and riches by these same means today. We could worship God and He can give us wealth and riches. And we could serve Him, and He can give us wealth and riches. When God does this, He is not being any different from us, the humans. We do so for our livelihood. If God continues to do this, He will not be any different from the devil.

But God devised a better plan: He gave us all the kingdoms and their splendor through Christ even before we worshiped or served or asked Him. They are ours whether we worship or serve Him or not. It is called

GRACE.[17] The only response God wants from us is to worship Him out of love, not duty or service – and giving Him thanks for all the wealth and riches He has already given us in Christ. That's our position.

APPLICATION:

God's wealth and riches have been judicially given to us in the heavenly places: "Praise be to the God and Father of our Lord Jesus Christ, who has blessed us in the heavenly realms with every spiritual blessing in Christ."[18] What this means is that God has already made a judicial determination that all wealth and riches are ours. But a judicial pronouncement is useless if we don't carry out a procedural requirement. That is, if we don't take the judgment and implement it. To translate God's judgment into reality (from spiritual to

[17] For a comprehensive discussion on GRACE, read, Charles Mwewa, *Law & Grace: An Expository Study in the Rudiments of Sin and Truth* (Ottawa: ACP, 2021)
[18] Ephesians 1:3

material), we need to:

(1) Think-up wealth-making ideas;

(2) Learn and understand how wealth works;

(3) Actually engage in money-making ventures (working or conducting businesses or investing);

(4) Be diligent and persistent (not giving up easily, no matter how many times we try – yes, sometimes you may have a warrant for something and still struggle to implement it!); and

(5) Be smart, including studying, observing, risk-taking (faith), and acquiring money-management skill-sets.

CAVEAT:

Satan has not spared even God's children when it comes to enticement for wanton gain. The true measure of riches and wealth from God is that it is harmless – it adds no pain or sorrow: "The blessing of the LORD makes a person rich, and he adds no sorrow with it."[19]

[19] Proverbs 10:22

6 GIFT AND EVERYTHING

"A person's gift opens doors for him, bringing him access to important people," *(Proverbs 18:16).*

There are five points to take home:

1. A gift will get you in to see anyone: Everyone is born with something the world wants (and sometimes, even needs). Discover that something within you.

2. A man's gift enlarges him, and seats him among princes [important people]. Your perfected gift will enlarge you and make you big. The world has a weakness; it favors talent, ability and resourcefulness, and sometimes, at the expense of character or morality. To get to the great people, develop your

gifts and that makes you visible and big. That way, you will both be attractive and you will attract the great. So, perfect (or develop) your gift.

3. A man's gift makes room for him and brings him before great men: The world has no room for normal, invisible people. In fact, the world takes advantage of such people, using them for its own purpose and then discarding them. You do yourself no favors by remaining average and normal. Discover your gift; perfect it; use it to make yourself big; and it will instantly create room for you. There is always room for gifted people or people who contribute something or are a gift to the world.

4. Do you want to meet an important person? Take a gift and it will be easy. There are two meanings to gift: One, it's the dominant, God-given talent

you were born with. And two, it can be a physical gift. Both have the same effects on important people – they make great people do something for you.

5. Important people make it easier for you to get what you want. If all you have are people at your level, you cannot rise higher than your level. Important people will provide you with connections less important people don't have.

LESSON:

In this world, there are people who have more of something – money, power, connections and influence. We call these people important or great people. They can be a president, a boss, a rich tycoon, a person with a higher position, a famous person, a connected person, a person with an historic name, a person with a recognizable talent, and so on. The more people have all these things the more they seek others with potential or gifts. To be attracted by these people, work on developing your gifts and it will open doors for you and make you big and visible.

Access to important people does the following:

(1) Makes it easier for you to make progress because of easy connections;

(2) Creates favor for you;

(3) You are assumed, meaning that other stages of interview or approval or testing are eliminated or waived;

(4) Positions you to begin at that high level; and

(5) Equates you to important people.

APPLICATION:

Great people are not gods and they may not always give us everything we want or need. However, important people usually occupy very important positions and have been granted some power to make official decisions that affect people. Such very important people may be in a position to recognize talents or gifts and open doors or put them to good use. Indeed, "A man's gift opens doors for him and brings him before great men."[20]

CAVEAT:

"For man sees the outward appearance, but the LORD sees the heart."[21] Please don't ignore or misunderstand this injunction. Both parts are important. Man sees the outward appearance – so, display yourself to be seen by people. If you make yourself invisible, you will be a nobody as far as this world is

[20] Proverbs 18:16
[21] 1 Samuel 16:7

concerned. God looks at the heart – when dealing with God, your outward appearance doesn't matter but your heart does. So, give to Caesar (man) what is man's (what he can see); and give to God what is God's (heart). You will then be successful both with men and with God.

7 MONEY OR NOTHING

"...money is the answer for everything,"
(Ecclesiastes 10:19).

There are five points to take home:

1. Money is a legal tender. This means that money is the acceptable medium of payment recognized by a legal system and is a legitimate way for meeting valid financial obligations. In a money economy, every nation has coins or banknotes that must be accepted whenever they are offered in payment for liabilities.

2. Money is a medium of exchange. This means that money is an intermediary instrument or system which is legally accepted to exchange it for goods and services. If you

have money, you can exchange it with any good or service you want.

3. Money bears intrinsic value for exchange. This means that the value of money you have can only purchase an equal value in goods or services. The more money you have, the more goods and services you can get. The less money you have, the less things you can get. If you have no money, you cannot exchange or get anything of some value.

4. Solomon wrote this statement, i.e., "Money answers all things," in reference only to the world (the earth) or "under the sun" – "I observed everything going on under the sun, and really, it is all meaningless—like chasing the wind."[22] This principle or observation, therefore, does

[22]Ecclesiastes 1:14

not apply to spiritual or heavenly economics. It is only an earthly, but not a heavenly, principle.

5. On earth, here in this world, "under the sun," presently in the order of the current economic setup, you need money to achieve earthly glories and accumulate things.

LESSON:

You will always need money to get the things of the value that you desire. Therefore,

(1) Make making money your priority;

(2) Because you need money to exchange with anything of value, make it a goal to study and know how money works and how to get more of it;

(3) If you make less money, do not desire things of more value than the

money you have or make. If you have more money, get the things you desire because you can afford them. In other words, be content in whichever financial situation you are;

(4) Government should ensure that every citizen has a means of earning or making money (jobs or businesses) – it must create a legislative environment that favors everyone to make some money; and

(5) Because money answers everything, work hard and be creative to acquire better money-making ideas. Money may be expensive but finding ways of making it is cheap and free.

APPLICATION:

Money may give everything – but that may not mean that everything money gives is good for you. It is, therefore, wise, to only use your money to exchange for those things that are good, valuable to you and others, or have eternal value.

8 SLAVE OF ONE MASTER

"You cannot be the slave of two masters! You will like one more than the other or be more loyal to one than the other. You cannot serve both God and mammon,"
(Matthew 6:24).

There are five points to take home:

1. Mammon means money, wealth or riches. In this context, money or mammon is regarded as people's attitude towards money, specifically, where money is regarded as an evil influence or an object of worship or devotion. It, in this sense, always depicts the demon of greed, covetousness or a voracious pursuit of gain.

2. Money or wealth or riches is neutral. Nowhere in the Bible does it say that money is bad or good. It is always your

attitude or approach towards it which is a subject of money in the Bible. For example, we read, "For the love of money is a root of all kinds of evil…"[23] Not money itself, but one's attitude towards it – "the LOVE of money," not the possession of money, or the accumulation of wealth – is what makes money enslave you or breed all kinds of evil in and through you.

3. Masters have slaves or servants WORKING for them. It is not the name "master" that makes you their slave, it is how the master relates you to their work that makes you his or her slave. If someone bought you to work for them, you are their slave. Even if someone did not buy you, but if they command or require you to work for them without pay or without adequate pay (unless there is

[23] 1 Timothy 6:10

an agreement to the contrary or it's a gratuitous relationship), then you are their slave.

4. A slave is owned or totally depends on the master. A slave serves (works) for the master under a strict and restrictive code. The slave has neither rights nor liberties; he is a perpetual prisoner. He is worse than a criminal, at least criminals reserve some rights and freedoms within their confinements.

5. The only way a slave can be free from the master is when the master dies, the master sells him to another enslaver, the slave escapes, the slave dies or the slave buys back his freedom or wins it through a fight/combat. If a master dies, a slave may be "inherited" by the master's successor. If the slave is sold to another enslaver, the slave is still a

slave. If the slave escapes, he could be arrested and the penalty may be death; and if the slave dies, he is dead (others may claim that this is ultimate freedom). The best is to buy back his freedom or win it through combat. That way, he is free here and now and becomes equal to his former master.

LESSON:

God is a better master than money. If God "enslaves" you, He, in fact, gives you back real freedom – freedom to live without fear, to inherent eternal life, to worship Him, and to love and be loved. If money enslaves you, it binds you to worry, to stress and fear of losing it. The more you are enslaved by God, the more loving, caring, generous, hopeful, helpful and liberated you become. The more you are enslaved by money, the more lost, greedy, impetuous, frivolous, callous, avaricious, pompous, proud and useless you become. A slave of God is richer than a slave of money.

APPLICATION:

First, if money is your master, God will be less important to you and eventually you may lose your soul.

Second, if God is your master, you will be less inclined to be controlled by people and money. Money will serve (work for) you.

Third, do not let another man or woman enslave you – not as a marital or sex slave or a labor slave, a house slave, a church slave, an industrial slave, a corporate slave, an academic slave, a mental/psychological slave, a social slave, a political slave (cadre), slave of the government or the media, or any form of slavery.

Fourth, work hard to acquire wealth – but then do to it what makes snakes useless, remove both its fangs and venomous pouch – give it away to the poor, the needy, the vulnerable and similarly-situated projects. If money is held on to tightly and ravenously, it becomes your master. If money is given away for good causes, it becomes your slave.

And fifth, have only one Master (God), and demand to be equal with everyone else – neither man nor the devil or money should be your master.

9 WORK INTELLIGENCE

"For even when we were with you, we gave you this rule: 'The one who is unwilling to work shall not eat'" (2 Thessalonians 3:10).

There are five points to take home:

1. The world, the earth or life dies when it is not worked. Work ensures continuity.

2. Food, similarly, ensures continuity. So, where there is no work, food will either be scarce or non-existent.

3. Food is a prerogative (an entitlement) of those who work. Only those who are not willing to work should not eat. Those who are willing to work (even if at the moment they don't have work) should eat.

4. The one who works longer, harder, more diligent, should be rewarded more and should eat more, and should feed on good food. Similarly, a hard worker deserves a good rest.

5. A lazy person should not also eat or should be denied food. Laziness and poverty are related; usually a poor person is also a person who is not willing to work longer or harder.

LESSON:

No matter where you live or how poor you were born, hard work will position you to move from your poverty status to well-off. There is nothing like a permanently poor place or person; there is only a place where people are perpetually lazy to manipulate their environment (work) to create food. No matter how much you wish or how strong you pray, if you don't work, you will die from hunger. To have good result, work must be joined to wisdom: If you work hard to cut a tree without fruits on it, even if you succeed in making it fall, there will still be no food on it. You would have wasted your energy (work). So, choose where you should exert your energy (work) to achieve the best outcome (food).

APPLICATION:

First, it is not the role of government to provide food to the people; government should only promote an environment where everyone can find or create work and make their own food.

Second, it is the role of every parent to provide food for their minor children (to children 16 or 17 years and below). It is not the responsibility of parents to feed their adult children (those 18 years and above). All adult children should be willing to work and fend for their own food.

Third, government should not deny food to any citizen who is willing to work – but government should not provide food to any adult citizen who is not willing to work.

Fourth, if anyone has work or is willing to work but spends all their money or resources on pleasure, beer or drugs, girlfriends or boyfriends or on gambling, they should be denied food as well.

And fifth, those who are willing to work or who work but do their jobs poorly, carelessly or without any regard to quality or excellence, they should be allowed to eat, with conditions. Such as if you don't work hard the next time, you will not be given free food. Or if your work continues to be substandard or of poor quality, you will not be given food or your job will be terminated.

10 EMPEROR, GOD AND A COIN

"Then Jesus told them, 'Give the Emperor what belongs to him and give God what belongs to God.' The men were amazed at Jesus" (Mark 12:17).

There are five points to take home:

1. Politics, law and religion: These three are among the central classifications in the world.

2. These systems, together, ensure earthly (worldly) survival and stability.

3. God uses them all – to run His affairs and govern the conducts of men and women on earth.

4. What happens in one, directly or indirectly, affects what

happens in the other.

5. All three are recognized in Scripture as authentic, powerful and essential to human experience. For example, God is said to exhibit all three in one: "For the LORD is our judge, the LORD is our lawgiver, the LORD is our king; it is he who will save us."[24] In other words, God is a Government (with Separation of Powers); Judge (or Judiciary); Lawgiver (or Legislature); and King (or Executive). God (religion) gives his commands (law) and He governs or rules (politics).

LESSON:

There is God on one end and politics/law on the other. You are directly involved or controlled or affected or expected to be part of one or both. You cannot be free from

[24] Isaiah 33:22

either or both all your days of your life. It does not matter whether you belong to one or both, you are a part of one of them, you are affected by all of them. If you chose to know or to ignore, it does not change the order of things.

APPLICATION:

First, politics, law or religion – in whichever you belong, you should consider it your calling.

Second, you cannot disparage or despise one and love the other.

Third, God will not reward one more than the other – they are co-equal in importance before God.

Fourth, in whichever you belong, glorify God.

And fifth, perform your obligations to each one according to what each demands: Thus, pay taxes to the emperor (government) and obey its laws – at the same time, love God and obey His commands. You cannot do one while avoiding the other.

11 WISE SERPENTS, INNOCENT DOVES

"Behold, I am sending you as lambs among wolves; be therefore crafty as snakes and innocent as doves," (Matthew 10:16).

There are five points to take home:

1. Nature of our present world: It is a rough world, filled with intrigue, subtleness, problems, troubles and all kinds of challenges. But it is also filled with goodness, joys and pleasures. Survival in this world is not automatic, you have to understand your world to thrive in or dominate it.

2. Every challenge or joy you will encounter in the world is already represented in one of God's created fauna or flora. This means that there is no

challenge on earth we cannot conquer. To do so, we just have to study a particular animal, bird's characteristics.

3. Two sets of animals' examples: There is a duo, unavoidable relationships that exists in the world: You're either a wolf or a lamb, a hunter or the hunted, a victor or the victim, a winner or loser, a champion or the vanquished, and etc. Unfortunately, that is both the nature and experience of life on earth.

4. To defeat life's challenges, you must observe and learn from nature – that's, how certain animals and vegetation live, thrive and survive.

5. Two creatures are particularly interested and were chosen and used by Jesus strategically: A snake and a dove. These two have identical strengths and weaknesses but in reverse to

each other. In particular:

A Snake:

a) The normal genius IQ is about 160. The snake's IQ may reach 180.

b) The snake is intelligent because it has a strong facet for remembering (a cobra, for example, will never forget its captor).

c) A snake can easily recognize its geographical boundaries.

d) A snake is rarely motivated by things that animals would kill for, such as food or light; a snake is motivated by darkness and silence – and these are things most animals are vulnerable in. Thus, a snake is nearly invisible, it is camouflaged by design so it can blend in almost all environments. When a snake moves into a new environment, it has the most patience to study, understand and learn its environment – to situate opportunities and dangers before it does anything (You may be living with a snake for years and you will never know that it has existed all this time).

e) A snake is a fast learner and has almost the same learning abilities as humans – so it can easily conquer you by learning your habits and anticipating. A snake has a penchant for solving puzzles, natural mazes and this is apparent in its movements.

f) A snake is the most elusive, sneaky and sly animal, as such it can easily escape and navigate complicated systems, terrains or situations.

g) A snake is the only animal that can renew its own life by shedding/sloughing its old skin – this is, thus, seen as a sign of eternity, fertility, rebirth, transformation, immortality, and healing. Just with all the hatred people have for snakes, but a snake has survived and continues to increase in numbers.

h) A snake is very prudent, careful, cunning, discerning, thoughtful, intelligent, sensible, sensitive and very creative. That is, it can at will invent a strategy even when cornered.

i) A snake is a meticulous thinker and swift decider – that's, it invests more time in thinking through an idea and acts very quickly to take action, before another takes it. In other words, a snake knows when to seize the moment and strike.

j) A snake has two undesirable qualities: Because of the above qualities, a snake can easily out-think, hoodwink, outsmart and deceive anyone. And also, a snake is lethally poisonous. It has the mind (cognition), and the venom (biological attribute), to accomplish its missions.

A Dove:

a) A dove is considered to be a clean creature (bird). It is a symbol of purity. It is usually used in sacrifices.

b) A dove is used as a symbol of peace. It is one of the most innocent creatures God has ever made.

c) A dove is gentle and compassionate. It is a symbol of love.

d) A dove is known as the, "Sheep of the bird world," because of its soft, gentle appearance and disposition.

e) A dove is a timid, trembling, and frightened bird.

f) A dove is too trusting of humans and is easily entrapped or snared.

g) A dove is a symbol of fairness and goodness. If sent on errands, it delivers as instructed.

h) A dove is a symbol of mourning – because of its low and soft cooing sound.

i) A dove has two weaknesses: Indecision and vacillation: It flies to and from and it seems disillusioned and disoriented in regards to its destiny. In other words, a dove is accused of lacking in commitment.

j) And the second weakness is that a dove can easily be deceived and is in need of a deliverer or deliverance.

OBSERVATION:

Human beings are the only creatures that can exhibit multi-quality excellencies animals and vegetation can only exhibit in exclusivity. For example, the grass is green, lions roar, roses may have many species but each can only display one permanent color, and etc.

But humans can choose to wear red, green, or blue at will. Or humans can choose to roar, screech, or hiss at will. Or humans can choose to change their habitation at will. Or humans can choose to change their preferences at will. What about a chameleon – all it can change are colors and nothing else. And humans can choose to study and imitate nature's techniques and strategies and apply such to their own lives.

LESSON:

In this lesson, we are being invited to experience life in balance, if we are to survive and be wise. We are implored to exhibit and understand the qualities of a snake, on one hand. And to display the qualities of a dove, on the other.

We must know:

(1) That shrewdness has its place in life.

(2) That innocence also has its place in life.

(3) Shrewdness by itself is dangerous.

(4) That innocence alone is a weakness.

(5) That to overcome the challenges and issues of life, we need to be both – as serpents (shrewd) and as doves

(innocent).

(6) That shrewdness, though useful, in extreme, however, is a quality best tempered by innocence.

(7) That if we lose this balance, we will become vulnerable to the world's volatility, machinations and ruthlessness. Without this balance, we are vulnerable to the system and others as a lamb is vulnerable to a wolf.

INSIGHT:

A snake is not a devil. The devil is called a serpent because he simply understands the qualities of a snake well and he uses them with practical precision. The devil, though, is unbalanced. He is skilled, smart, decisive, creative, sneaky, and etc., but he is not innocent, loving, peaceful, nor considerate. By observing a snake and a dove, we can match any shrewdness and also neutralize its deleterious effects. With this balance, we can win in every sphere of life.

12 HONESTY, BREAD & BUTTER

"The master commended the dishonest manager because he had acted shrewdly. For the people of this world are shrewder in dealing with their own kind than are the people of the light," (Luke 16:8).

There are five points to take home:

1. When it comes to this world we live in, being smart in dealing with people, is supreme.

2. Position without possession may be meaningless. In world economics, position must also bring possession. When you have a position (job, business, politics, church, and etc.), build a house, buy property, accumulate the nice things of life for yourself and your children (leave an inheritance), and etc.

3. Honesty is currency, but only if it can protect your possessions. If you are honest and you lose, you are still a winner. But be careful that you don't act honestly but unwisely.

4. Shrewdness is king – the ability to predict human nature and behavior and take appropriate steps to guard yourself or protect your possession.

5. Jesus said that Christians may be weak in using their brains and minds in this world; that's why they fail to compete favorably with the world in creating wealth and gathering possessions. That should change.

LESSON:

Whether you like it or not, you are first born into this world (and are impacted by what goes on in this world) before you are born into God's family. To succeed in this world, be shrewd (astute, sharp, smart, perceptive, intelligent and discerning).

APPLICATION:

If you want to win a political election and you are a conservative Christian, do not dwell on your faith much until you win the election. That way the people of the world (who are the majority voters) will give you their vote.

If you are a Christian business person, study business trends, markets, accounting, marketing, profit hubs, and etc. and do not relegate everything to "simply praying."

If you have skeletons in your past, don't share with your enemy who will only dagger you while you are falling.

If you want to marry the most beautiful woman or the most handsome man, make a strategy and woo them to you, of course, in good faith.

If you are poor and don't have money, make friends with the rich, the powerful and the influential who will give you a way to the corners of wealth and power – if you mingle only with those who are struggling like you, you will be both dead in few days.

ADVICE:

After you conquer the world using its own weapons, then use your gift, connections, power, position, wealth, properties, possessions and influence, spiritually, to advance the Kingdom of God.

13 EQUAL PAY, EQUAL VALUE

"So, I said, 'Wisdom is better than strength.' But the poor man's wisdom is despised, and his words are no longer heeded," (Ecclesiastes 9:16).

There are five points to take home:

1. Both wisdom and strength (power, influence, or abilities) are good. But wisdom is better.

2. Wisdom creates your strategy and tactics; strength brings about the victory, the spoils.

3. Thinking (wisdom) before you do (action, strength) is the best policy, anywhere, everywhere, and it ensures that your victories are sustainable and lasting.

4. Both poor and rich people

may have wisdom. But the rich may have better resources to translate them into victorious results.

5. The wisdom of the poor is silenced by the wealth and influence of the strong and powerful.

LESSON:

There is no intrinsic value in being poor because the resultant end is to benefit the rich, the wealthy or the powerful. So, the poor can do only one thing with their wisdom: If the poor person has wisdom, the poor person MUST sell their wisdom to the rich who have need for it and also the means to purchase it.

Life revolves around fair exchange. The rich may have need for wisdom. The poor will have need for money. Both have what the other lacks. The wise thing to do is to transact through fair exchange of what each possesses.

The debacle has always been in the rich setting unfair brokerage and unfair conditions (unfair advantage). over the poor. Consider, for example, a poor country like Zambia but which is very rich in the mineral of copper. Rich, industrialized countries need copper for electrical wiring as well as for making jewelry. The rich may not give the poor country a fair bargaining, leading to the poor becoming poorer and the rich getting richer.

The poor need to trade very intelligently with their wisdom or resources. They ought to diversify not only their wisdom (resources) but whom they trade with as well. In that way, they may leverage the prospects and maximize their profits.

APPLICATION:

You may serve or help a powerful person win or achieve greatly, but in the end, you will be forgotten and dumped. Therefore, make sure that they (the rich, powerful, strongmen) pay you for the value of your wisdom (words, contributions), and anything less than that may be unwise.

14 ROCK WISDOM

"Rock badgers: they are not a mighty people, but they make their homes in the rocks,"
(Proverbs 30:26).

There are five points to take home:

1. Rock badgers – they are a "people", just like us (humans). A way of saying that they are susceptible to similar dangers and weaknesses as humans.

2. Rock badgers (also known as dassies or *pimbi*, *pelele* and *wibari* or rock rabbit or conies, or hyraxes), are feeble, not mighty, not strong, weak, or lacking in power. That's what nature has given to them – their weakness. That, they can't change. They are made as

a weak creature.

3. The rock badgers live in, or among the rocks, their choice of habitation.

4. The rock badgers are hunted or preyed upon by leopards, Egyptian cobras, puff adders, rock pythons, caracals, wild dogs, hawks, and owls. These predators all have one thing in common: They are stronger, relatively larger and capable of killing the rock badgers without difficulty.

5. The rock badgers chose the rocks for strategic advantage. All of its predators, although relatively larger and vicious and even venomous, they struggle with the rocks or are too large to navigate the rock crevices, and mostly exhibit the Savannah and rain forests. And for the three types of snakes which prey upon them, although they are found in

rocks, these predators are large and do not effectively penetrate the rocks. In that sense, the choice of rocks as their habitation, is the safest and most secure place to dwell for the rock badgers.

LESSON:

To survive on earth:

First, know and understand your weakness (know who you are, what you are capable of, and what you are not able to do).

Second, know the characteristics of your enemy – those who seek your defeat (the devil, bad people or the environment you live in and etc.).

Third, choose your place wisely – where you can maximize safety, wealth-creation and even favor.

And fourth, for example, if you are marrying, choose a partner who completes you, complements your weaknesses or is strong where you are weak, and *vice versa*; or choose a career you can do within the strength make-up of your being; choose the means of making money that, within your abilities, provides the best returns, and etc.

APPLICATION:

God has given each person or creature something to overcome their limitations, flaws, faults, weaknesses, or disadvantages. No-one can blame God for their failings – all they need is to consider the rock badgers and make the right, strategic and thought-through choices. It's not too late to learn and apply, "Rock Wisdom."

15 LOCUST LOGIC

"Locusts have no king, yet they advance together in ranks," (Proverbs 30:26).

There are five points to take home:

1. Everyone knows the effectiveness of their missions – when locusts land, they archive their purpose with precision; they devastate whatever they target. Locusts are effective.

2. Locusts always move in the same direction, together.

3. Locusts have no king, no ruler, no leader – but they all move in the same direction. How do they do that? They have sectional "commanders" and these command in tune together and with no overall

leader, they know exactly where to go, when to go, and when to retreat.

4. Locusts advance together in ranks – that is, they know where each belong and they don't break their ranks. They don't envy any other ranks; they don't covet each other. They advance (make progress) together, as a leaderless team.

5. Locusts exemplify group-purpose, collective wisdom, and systematic synergy. They demonstrate "unity" and not "union."

LESSON:

One characteristic defines every system; it's its predictability and order. A secure system has reached maturation whereby things work in a predictable, unbreakable way. Thus, human element is only necessary to provide or sustain solidarity. A good system is not based on one individual or a group of individuals to function. It is not a rule of men. The System[25] can survive even when humans fail or expire. It has in-built strength to withstand chaos or lack of good leadership.

Where there is an effective system, leaders are secondary. Without a system, anyone person (a leader) can become too strong and manipulate (dictate over) others. The System ensures equality – where everyone is equal regardless of rank within their respective quadrants.

For example, some African nations have not achieved the "Locust Logic." They are still a "One Strong Man Rule," – where one man, usually a president, dictates and determines all national transactions. Similarly, nations still under "blood rule" or rule by the so-called royal families, cannot

---

[25] A book by this author titled, *The System* (Ottawa: ACP, 2021) covers comprehensively the rudiments of the three quadrants of the Makers, Maintainers and Grinders.

boast of championing the Locust Logic. Nations should not accept the fact that only one individual or a group of individuals or one family has the mandate to rule and others don't.

Another example, most marriages can be happy where only if both partners are equal, but each knows their "rank" and walk in it without usurping the other. Or two friends can succeed in one enterprise (partnership) without each trying to beat or hoodwink the other.

APPLICATION:

An important reason why the Locust Logic is needed, is that, where there is a system, goals, visions, businesses, enterprises, governance or dreams, do not die with the death of the strong leader – things continue the same way and progress.

16 LIZARDS AND SPIDERS

"Lizards—they are easy to catch, but they are found even in kings' palaces," + "The spider skillfully grasps with its hands, and it is in kings' palaces," (Proverbs 30:28).

There are five points to take home:

1. Lizards are common and are easy to find and catch – that's their weakness.

2. Just like most of us, we are not born with influence, power or connections. Sometimes, we are simple and very accessible.

3. Lizards are found in kings' palaces – that is, they know two things:

   (a) How to make important connections

(b) How to rise in ranks

4. Spiders have only one strength – grasping with their hands.

5. With only that one skill, spiders are able to reach and abide in kings' palaces.

LESSON:

Your birth, name or background does not matter – you don't need to be already powerful or influential or wealthy to make it to the top. You don't need many skills, either. Use the one skill (hands, and etc.) that God has given you and weave your way to the top with it.

APPLICATION:

There is a difference between data and information. Data is raw, information is processed. Few people know how to use information. They are perpetual students who are puffed up with knowledge. But they don't know how to use it. Information is a resource, the more of it you have, the more powerful you are.

There are many people "liking" various thoughts and ideas people post on Facebook, and others twitting and retweeting interesting issues on Twitter. However, for most people, it ends just there, on liking or retweeting. One would have thought that with such free and rare information being presented people would make use of it and change their situations. Alas, majority still remain the same.

Governments, leaders, businesses and inventors spend enormous amounts of money to purchase information. They would not do so if it were not profitable. The more access to information you have, the more, relatively, your life should change. Like lizards, they are easily caught, but they can easily enter palaces or centers of power. Both the spider and the lizard have one thing in common, they use their skills to move up – to establish their residence in palaces.

Jesus lamented on the quality, and not the quantity of people's expectations or faith: "He answered, Because of your little faith [your lack of trust and confidence in the power of God]; for I assure you and most solemnly say to you, if you have [living] faith the size of a mustard seed, you will say to this mountain, 'Move from here to there,' and [if it is God's will] it will move; and nothing will be impossible for you."[26] The quality of your belief is more important than the quantity.

You do not need too much information, too much teaching, too much learning, too much coaching, too much preparation, or too much evidence. All you need is the quality of anything, and you can move mountains or enter into kings' palaces. The Holy Bible calls it "earnest expectation."[27] That's all you need .

---

[26] Matthew 17:20 (Amplified Bible)
[27] Romans 8:19

17 THESE LITTLE ANTS

"Ants are creatures of little strength, yet they store up their food in the summer," *(Proverbs 30:25).*

There are five points to take home:

1. Ants are creatures – just like us (humans). In that regard, they are not different from us.

2. Ants have little strength – that is their weakness. If they want, they can dwell on their weakness and die. But they can do something instead of merely complaining.

3. "They…store up…food…" – ants know that they have little strength. But they also know that there is strength in numbers. So, they team up to achieve a huge task, storing up

food in the summer. What they can't achieve individually, ants know, is possible through team-work.

4. The most important need ants have is food. They can't store it in inclement weather or seasons. They choose to work in good months of summer to get food ready for wintry and windy seasons. If they sleep or play hard in "work-season," they can't reap the benefits in "harvest-season."

5. Ants have wisdom to read the times and to prepare using collective strength. Failure to do so, may mean the end of their existence.

LESSON:

God has given each person or creature something to offset their weaknesses so that they can survive. Every creature should discover what is its advantage and use it appropriately to survive.

APPLICATION:

For anything that succeeded greatly, preparation was key. And we see this right in the first book of the Bible: "Now the earth was formless and void, and darkness was over the surface of the deep. And the Spirit of God was hovering over the surface of the waters. And God said, 'Let there be light,' and there was light."[28] In these verses of the Scriptures one can hear the gap and feel the genuine space. It is one of those styles of language that says so many things in few sentences. You can see God preparing, and when He acts, it is a brilliant light. This is within us; we are made in the image of God.[29]

---

[28] Genesis 1:3

[29] See Genesis 1:27:

The ants seem to understand the ABC of conquest:

1. First – acknowledge your weakness or limitation.

2. Second – believe in who you are.

3. And third – conquer your limitations through preparation.

Acknowledge your limitation. It could be your lack of confidence, your lack of education or lack of knowledge, or your physical limitations (height, weight, color, and etc.) Believe in who you are. Doubting yourself or trying to be like someone else will not do it. Take pride in what you have and who you are.

Embrace your limitations, love who you are – in fact, that is the second commandment, to love yourself: "The second is this: 'Love your neighbor as yourself.' There is no commandment greater than these."[30]

You can't love your neighbor if you don't love yourself. That will be hypocritical. So, celebrate who you are – your physical features, your mannerisms, your approach to life and everything about you.

Compare to no-one and to nothing. You are one of your own kind, you are in the class of your own. And that is the truth. Believe it. Conquer your limitations through preparation. If you lose, turn your loss into investments. Never quit but turn your resignation into vacation. And never stop preparing until someday you reach your ultimate destination.

And note this, if you want to climb the tallest tree, people will react to you in three stages: Before you climb, they will say, "No-one has ever conquered it." When you climb half way, they will say, "No-one has ever finished."

---

[30] Mark 12:31

And when you reach the top, they will say, "It's so easy, anyone can do it." From the beginning, have the *top-of-the-tree mentality*, for whatever project or challenge you have, say, "It's so easy I can do it."

18 FALLING TO RISE

"For though the righteous fall seven times, they rise again, but the wicked stumble when calamity strikes," (Proverbs 24:16).

There are five points to take home:

1. There are three assumptions noted in this verse of Scripture: The first is that being righteous doesn't preclude one from trouble. In fact, our Lord said, "I have told you these things, so that in me you may have peace. In this world you will have trouble. But take heart! I have overcome the world."[31]

2. The second assumption is that the righteous do fall.

3. The third assumption is that "seven" seems to be the

[31] John 16:33

minimum the righteous might fall.

4. The three assumptions, collectively, indicate that the matter is not in falling (because that is obvious), but in rising up each time they fall.

5. And righteous' fall is real; it is not a mere stumble or a near-fall.

LESSON:

Bad things do happen to good people. And good things do happen to bad people. That is a true rule of nature. Troubles, problems, and negative experiences do not mean that you are wrong, sinning or not loved by God. Those who love God do suffer from the same hardships as those who don't know God. The calamities that befall the unrighteous also befall the righteous.

The bad things happening to you don't mean that you are out of favor with God. When God allows something bad or negative to happen to you, it is because He has a purpose for it. The fact that you are in trouble more than once or twice or even seven times, doesn't mean that God has forsaken you, either. As we have read, the righteous can fall, but they will rise up. Sometimes falling is the clearest indication that God is with you.

Adam fell, but God provided him with a covering. Abraham fell, but God sustained him and gave him a son with Sarah. Joseph fell, but God brought him up and he became Egypt's Prime Minister. Moses fell, but God rescued him and relaunched him in Egypt. Samson fell, but his hair grew again. David fell, but he reclaimed his throne. Our Lord Jesus died, but God raised Him up on the third day. Some of Jesus' disciples fell, but they stood up again and became God's apostles. Apostle Paul fell many times into the hands of city gangs and officials, but God rescued him every time.

The difference between the righteous and the unrighteous lies in how they handle pain, sufferings or hardships. The righteous see the purpose and plan of God in it and it doesn't destroy them. However, the unrighteous are destroyed simply by a mere stumble or a mere near-fall. The true power of righteousness is in the fact that not even death can destroy them.

APPLICATION:

The truth about suffering or pain is that it doesn't last forever; it is temporary. Most people fear to do the impossible because they fear pain. Everyone who has conquered pain, has defeated failure, disappointment, poverty and negative circumstances. The most precious gift on earth is human life, and every woman knows that it comes through pain. But women can also tell us that though painful, pain is temporary; it ends when the joy of life comes out. You can't move up or forward if you fear pain. Embrace pain, it is necessary to glory.

If you experience pain, suffering, hardships or very difficult situations, do the following:

(1) Give thanks: "Give thanks in all circumstances; for this is God's will for you in Christ Jesus."[32] "All circumstances," means all; and this includes in bad or uncomfortable circumstances.

(2) Rejoice in your suffering: "Not only that, but we also rejoice in our sufferings…"[33]

(3) Know that every suffering God allows, is a process towards another breakthrough: "…because we know that suffering produces perseverance; perseverance, character; and character,

---

[32] 1 Thessalonians 5:18

[33] Romans 5:3

hope."[34] We all may not approve or even like God's methods of doing things, but we surely love the results. No matter how painful the suffering experience was, the end result is always good. To God every suffering is like birth pangs; in the end, it produces something good.[35] All the pain and suffering God allows in your life, is a process towards something great. Embrace it and stay in there and endure to the end. You will be saved; literally, you will achieve.

(4) Know that God is working it out together for your good: "And we know that God causes all things to work together for good to those who love God, to those who

[34] *Ibid.*, verse 3b and 4

[35] See Matthew 24:8; Romans 8:21-31

are called according to His purpose."[36]

(5) Receive hope: "And hope does not put us to shame, because God's love has been poured out into our hearts through the Holy Spirit, who has been given to us."[37] At the end of the process, you will gain hope, and that hope will not disappoint, because when God is in control, He deals with you in love. Try to see your current pain or suffering in another light, as stepping stones towards your destiny. You will be better at the end.

Pains and sufferings are our allies. They are instruments for good. They are our vehicles to our notable destination. They are not meant to destroy us.

In Greek Mythology, a hero (a champion)'s journey passes

[36] Romans 8:28 (New American Standard Bible)
[37] Romans 5:5

through many trials and sufferings. He is called to take on the adventure. Then a supernatural being helps him on the journey. He then crosses the threshold or the unknown territory where he faces many enduring tests. He is assisted by mentors before he faces his ultimate trial. Successful negotiation of the trial brings him to his resolution or revelation. He is transformed. He atones for his sins and then he returns from the unknown to normal life.

Under Grace, we are more than conquerors: "No, in all these things we are more than conquerors through him who loved us."[38] Christ fought in the war and brought us the victory. However, Christ did not do away with our requirement to refine our character. That happens after suffering and

[38] Romans 8:37

perseverance. We are not expected to go back to the Cross. That was done for us. However, we are expected to withstand all the trials, hardships or sufferings we may encounter from time to time on our way to individual glory. Like well-trained stallions, we don't run away from trouble, we run towards trouble, and we conquer.

CAVEAT:

There are many times that people neglect or even run away from those who are suffering. This should not be. When someone is passing through turbulent situations in their life journey, they are closer to victory than those who supposedly have everything going on well for them.

Real champions, real winners become; they were forged out of trouble. We should rejoice and celebrate with those who are suffering. We should give them the necessary push and motivation. They are the true heroes.

INDEX

APPENDIX I

The Rich Man and Lazarus

[19] "There was a rich man who was dressed in purple and fine linen and lived in luxury every day. [20] At his gate was laid a beggar named Lazarus, covered with sores [21] and longing to eat what fell from the rich man's table. Even the dogs came and licked his sores.

[22] "The time came when the beggar died and the angels carried him to Abraham's side. The rich man also died and was buried. [23] In Hades, where he was in torment, he looked up and saw Abraham far away, with Lazarus by his side. [24] So he called to him, 'Father Abraham, have pity on me and send Lazarus to dip the tip of his finger in water and cool my tongue, because I am in agony in this fire.'

[25] "But Abraham replied, 'Son, remember that in your lifetime you received your good

things, while Lazarus received bad things, but now he is comforted here and you are in agony. [26] And besides all this, between us and you a great chasm has been set in place, so that those who want to go from here to you cannot, nor can anyone cross over from there to us.'

[27] "He answered, 'Then I beg you, father, send Lazarus to my family, [28] for I have five brothers. Let him warn them, so that they will not also come to this place of torment.'

[29] "Abraham replied, 'They have Moses and the Prophets; let them listen to them.'

[30] "'No, father Abraham,' he said, 'but if someone from the dead goes to them, they will repent.'

[31] "He said to him, 'If they do not listen to Moses and the Prophets, they will not be convinced even if someone rises from the dead.'"

ABOUT THE AUTHOR

CHARLES MWEWA

Charles Mwewa (LLM – cand.) is a Dad, a husband, a prolific author and researcher, poet, novelist, political thinker, a law professor, and Christian and community leader. Mwewa has written no less than 30 books and counting. Mwewa, his wife and their three daughters, reside in the Canadian Capital City of Ottawa.

AUTHOR'S CONTACT

Email Address:

spynovel2016@gmail.com

Facebook:

www.facebook.com/charlesmwewa

Twitter:

https://twitter.com/BooksMwewa

Instagram:

instagram.com/mwewabooks/?hl=en

Author's Website:

https://www.charlesmwewa.com

Made in the USA
Middletown, DE
26 September 2021